CW00656061

opening

POEMS

AND

SPACES

deborah fielding

© 2021 by Deborah Fielding

Published by St. Mark's MK
PO Box 7666, Milton Keynes, MK11 9PE
stmarksmk.com
Charity Number 1180087

Cover and design by Becky Hance
beckyhance.com

Printed in the United Kingdom on recycled paper

All rights reserved

9781739845209

For my family,

friends

and all the

other teachers,*

with thanks.

---

*See footnotes
and further reading

introduction

**Words are all we've got
to make sense of our stories.
So please be patient.**

When I was 21, a godmother, Joyce, gave me a dictionary.
Inside she wrote, 'Love to Debbie who has found and
resides in The Word.' I have still got it.

To some The Word refers to the written word generally.
To others it refers to both the Bible and to Jesus - Divine
Love in human form.* In this case, Joyce meant all of these.
Everything I write is about love.

I was brought up on and in prayer and with lots of books.

For many years I have written short fiction but the
pandemic and other events of 2020 and 2021 turned me
into a poet. I wrote to process all that I was consuming
and experiencing. Poems became digestive enzymes for my
thoughts and feelings.

*John 1:1-5

Poetry and prayer, for me, both come from rich honesty and reach out into mystery. Both ask questions and name experiences, both can contain pain, fear and anger and neither have to be over-complicated or 'correct'. Both can have form, but there are no rules.

I first fell in love with writing in my third year of university because I realised I could do anything with it. I have learned that prayer can be anything too - and it's not confined to the page. I first fell in love with prayer after a long illness. I borrowed before I could produce my own.

In this book, you will find first a series of thoughts and questions, followed by a collection of short poems all written between March 2020 and November 2021. The poems follow the three line, seventeen-syllable form, sometimes called modern haiku.*

I like to write using the brief modern haiku form because it forces me to make a point, create a punchline, or crystallise an idea. But I have never felt comfortable with being explicit. I don't like to nail down important things in case I disfigure them. Or more particularly, trap them. Ideas belong in the open.

---

*These are very different from traditional haiku or hokku, a Japanese form which was the opening of a longer poem (renga) often juxtaposing a pair of seasonal images - poetryfoundation.org

Some of these poems were written on my notes app on daily walks during lockdown, some in angry bursts after looking at the news on my phone, some respond to what I was reading or experiencing. I have attached footnotes to some, to give context, if you want it. I am constantly inspired by books, objects and people and you will find a list of further reading at the back. Do look up these writers and their valuable work as well as reading my personal interpretations.

I hope you will find the book useful. Perhaps you might find yourself on the pages - either in the poems or in the spaces. Or perhaps you might want to open up yourself and get out a pencil. I hope it gives you permission to stop in the face of Mystery.

Thank you so much for reading,

Deborah Fielding
November 2021

'Pray with open hand, not
with clenched fist.'

Lord Dunsany

prayers

It hurts.

I am sorry.

I am afraid.

I am angry.

I am tearful.

What can I do to help?

Why do some people die?

Why are some people really ill?

Why do some people get better?

What am I meant to do?

Why are so many people abandoned?

Why are people dishonest?

What did I do wrong?

Am I a good person?

poems

I've got a voice and
a furnace in my belly.
Weary, but ready.*

06/05/20

---

*Covid-19 hit the UK in March 2020. The
first lockdown took place between March
and July.

My white skin means that
I have never had to think
about my white skin.*

27/06/20

*On **"White Privilege: Unpacking the
Invisible Knapsack"** by Peggy McIntosh and
Me and White Supremacy by Layla F Saad,
in the wake of George Floyd's murder.

I'm breaking up with
perfectionism. We don't
have fun anymore.

07/07/20

Grief and hope play here
With my heart and with my strength.
There is no winner.

09/08/20

Bodies, thick with grief
for good ideas unlived,
demand attention.

09/08/20

There are tears inside
that cannot find their way out.
Together, we wait.

09/08/20

Disappointment means
that we hoped and that we tried.
That we were alive.

14/08/20

We need to re-learn
how to learn and make mistakes -
to be beginners.*

28/08/20

*On **The Next Right Thing,**
by Emily P. Freeman

Let's talk about it.
        Whatever it is, speak up.
        Let's not waste our time.

                        28/08/20

Words are all we've got
to make sense of our stories.
So please be patient.

28/08/20

The end of summer
means a return to the new.
New shoes on old ground.

30/08/20

How do we pray if
our bodies are clogged, slow, sad?
How do we pray then?

31/08/20

Help me to listen
    when I don't want to listen.
        Help me to be open.*

01/09/20

*On the work of Osheta Moore,
#DearWhitePeacemakers.

It's okay to cry.
Please cry when it hurts, because
then I can cry too.

01/09/20

We, called to justice -
        called to be truly loving.
        We must do something.*

                    02/09/20

*On the work of Danielle Coke.

I am still learning
to unlearn my biases.
Shame will do no good.*

04/09/20

*In response to anti-racism education.

Knowing better is
easy. Doing better is
horribly messy.*

07/09/20

*On activism.

Theory is easy.
There is no risk in knowledge.
Speaking up is hard.*

07/09/20

*More on activism.

We 'other' those who
'other' others. Thinking we
are superior.

07/09/20

This year I have found
that my anxiety is
social. No offence.

27/09/20

The one who tells you
to tense up or run away?
She is a scared child.*

19/09/21

*On **A Toolkit for Modern Life,**
Dr. Emma Hepburn

What is a body,
        but a way to feel ourselves
            alive in the world?*

02/10/20

*On Pilates.

She holds the details:
a tone, a breath, a mood change.
She captures it all.*

07/10/20

---

*Inspired by the work of
Nicola Rae-Wickham

We thought an open
invitation was enough.
It was not enough.*

08/10/20

---

*On inclusivity in the church
and elsewhere.

Is everyone
extremely aggravating,
or am I in pain?

17/10/20

Heads and hearts aching,
peering into the distance,
we look out for hope.*

31/10/20

---

*The second UK lockdown took place in
November 2020.

Kindness is not just
a superficial absence
of hatred. It's love.*

15/11/20

---

*On the popular hashtag #BeKind

I have loved fiercely,
        and it has hurt sometimes.
        That is what love is.

25/11/20

While I was busy
mending the broken bits. The
rest of me was fine.

25/11/20

Grief lives here, but not
quite alone. There are others.
Good companions.

31/12/20

This is all too much
all at once. So let's take it
one   *

05/01/21

---

*The third UK Lockdown took place
between January and April 2021.

Before unity
     we need justice and healing.
   We must tend the roots.*

                              24/01/21

---

*On the United States Inauguration,
January 2021.

God, we are tired.
Please help us to get some sleep.
Give us holy rest.

11/01/21

God, I am so cross.
Everything winds me up.
Please give me more grace.

02/02/21

If I think, 'I hope
so-and-so is okay,' am
I praying for them?

16/02/21

Beauty is bigger.
    Beautiful things help us out.
    They shrink our horrors.

23/02/21

When we are alone
and I cannot feel you near.
May I keep going.

02/03/21

Our breath is a tool
to heal and to release us.
Body and spirit.*

03/03/21

It is in our breath
that we can endure the pain.
And move it onwards.*

03/03/21

*More on Pilates.

Maybe I don't need
to attribute a meaning
to everything.

05/03/21

I do not fit in
    to those narrow spaces you
        leave. I am bigger.

08/03/21

In love, let's not hide
control inside protection.
May we empower.*

19/03/21

*On the fine line between protecting
women and other marginalised people
and controlling them, in the wake of Sarah
Everard's murder..

I don't want to die.
I'm human. I'm scared, I have
hopes and desires.*

03/21

---

*Matt 26:39
On Holy Week and Easter 2021

Try humans again.
They are messy, hurt, afraid.
We are beloved.*

03/21

*Luke 23:34
On Holy Week and Easter 2021

In death we are not
alone. Many are walking
on the road, with us.*

03/21

*Luke 23:43
On Holy Week and Easter 2021

Do not look away.
We belong to each other.
Start by listening.*

03/21

---

*John 19:26
On Holy Week and Easter 2021

You said you loved me.
But where are you now, in this?
Do you even care?*

03/21

---

*Matthew 27:46
On Holy Week and Easter 2021

In the midst of pain
comes the sense that things cannot
hurt this much again.*

03/21

*John 19:30
On Holy Week and Easter 2021

There is a beauty
in relinquishing control.
In being cared for.*

03/21

---

*Luke 23:48-56
On Holy Week and Easter 2021

In love, I am known.
I am worth more than I thought.
Abundance is here.*

03/21

*John 20:11-16
On Holy Week and Easter 2021

Don't sit in your shame,
or inside your certainties.
Rise, together. Live!*

03/21

They said you were good -
that you cared about us all.
Were they idiots?*

27/04/21

*Rage Prayers

All I've got is rage.
Rage and grief and frustration.
Where is your love now?*

27/04/21

*Rage Prayers

They quoted verses
with "promises" spelling hope.
But were those for me?*

27/04/21

---

*Rage Prayers

These tears in my throat
have been there for months and years.
Nobody wants them.*

27/04/21

*Rage Prayers

They sit and wonder,
        not looking ahead or back.
   There is beauty here.

03/05/21

I make myself small
to squeeze into their safety.
Remind me to grow.

04/05/21

I have become pinched.
I used to be generous
in my perceptions.

05/21

He could not subscribe
if it meant losing his sense
of self and control.*

07/21

*Mark 10:17-22

Everyone here
    deserves the very best now.
        Without exception.*

07/21

*John 2:1-11

After much heartbreak
abuse, pain and discomfort,
she trusted again.*

07/21

*Mark 5:21-43

The jar had been full
of fear, questions and regret.
She emptied it there.*

07/21

Their desperation
bred openness of spirit
and of family.*

07/21

*Mark 5:21-43

To wait and wait with
no guarantee of outcome.
Is that the real strength (love)?*

07/21

They walk away then,
      remembering their oneness
with the one they charge (hate?).*

07/21

---

*John 8:1-11

Why do we think in
      absolutes? We cannot live
        our lives in that way.

13/07/21

Why are we tearful
when we meet goodness in the
postman or cashier?

13/07/21

In recovery
we are free to do lovely
terrifying things.*

27/07/21

---

*On recovery of mental health.

There is a something
that moves in my skin and brain.
Something that's not me.

29/07/21

His prayer was answered.
Safe certainty made way for
daunting potential.*

07/21

You're too late for us.
There is nothing left inside.
Just leave us alone.*

07/21

She could stop at last
and find herself known and loved
in the same moment.[*]

07/21

---

*John 4:1-30

I have spent my life
building a safety system.
How can I trust this?*

07/21

Alone, he could do
nothing but struggle and wait
for the pain relief.*

07/21

*Mark 5:1-20

May I remember
my story is important –
but no more than yours.

11/08/21

The movies show how
to defeat enemies, but
not what to do next.

15/08/21

This is the murky
middle. It's too early yet
to taste the fruit. Wait.*

27/08/21

*Restrictions officially lifted in the UK in
June 2021, but COVID-19 is ongoing.

Before they were them,
there was an understanding.
A sense of joy.*

08/21

*Luke 1:39-45

They were introduced
in blood and shit and screaming.
There he meets us first.*

08/21

*Luke 2:7

I am on my knees
and you are on yours. Perhaps
I am not alone.

06/09/21

Time given warmly,
gently and expansively.
This is family.*

09/21

---

*Mark 10:13-16

What better way to
wake than with peace, health, food and
the face of loving.*

09/21

*Mark 5:21-43

When we recognise
    love in new place or person.
    We know to pursue.*

09/21

*Luke 5:1-11

It looks like magic
    when material change comes.
        Magic or something.*

                    09/21

*Luke 5:17-26

How are we meant to
    care for one with contrary
      desires and designs?*

                        09/21

There is nothing more
disconcerting than people
who mix with 'others.'*

09/21

---

*Luke 5:27-31

Giving your whole self
and people not wanting you.
It hurts all over.*

09/21

*Luke 4:14-30

It isn't simple,
the decision to give in.
It isn't simple.*

09/21

*Mark 14:10-11

If I want to have
more joy, more faith, more patience,
I will need some help.*

09/21

We can imagine
      that newness is closed to us.
            Before we look up.*

09/21

---

*Luke 2:8-14, Matt 2:9-12

Our lives narrow when
we persist in refusing
offerings of love.*

09/21

*John 5:1-15

There is ample space
here for grief and gratitude.
I am big enough.

11/10/21

It's okay to stop.
We cannot grow ceaselessly.
We're not parasites.*

01/11/21

*On **How to Do Nothing**, Jenny Odell

further reading

books

A Toolkit for Modern Life, Dr. Emma Hepburn
An Alter in the World and Learning to Walk in the Dark, Barbara Brown Taylor
Anti-Racist Ally, Sophie Williams
Black and British, David Olusoga
Celtic Daily Prayer Book Two, Northumbria Community Trust
Help, Thanks, Wow and Bird by Bird, Anne Lamott
Honest Advent, Scott Erickson
How to be a Craftivist, Sarah Corbett
Prayer and This Sunrise of Wonder, Michael Mayne
Selected Poems, R. S. Thomas
Seventeen Syllables, Lori Hetteen
The Bible, New Revised Standard Version
The Celtic Wheel of the Year, Tess Ward
The House on Mango Street, Sandra Cisneros
The Next Right Thing, Emily P. Freeman
The Path Between Us, Suzanne Stabile
The Power of Writing it Down, Allison Fallon
The Selected Poems and A Country of Marriage, Wendell Berry
Walking on Water, Madeleine L'Engle
What White People Can Do Next, Emma Dabiri

instagram

Brad Montague, writer, artist **@BradMontague**
Cole Arthur Riley, writer **@BlackLiturgies**
Danielle Coke, illustrator, advocate **@OhHappyDani**
I E, climate justice centering BIPOC voices **@IntersectionalEnvironmentalist**
Jeannie Di Bon, hypermobility expert, therapist **@Jeannie_Di**
Kalkidan Legesse, speaker, writer **@kalkidan.legesse.mekuria**
Kazvare, writer, illustrator **@KazvareMadeIt**
Marcie Alvis-Walker, writer **@BlackCoffeeWithWhiteFriends**
Morgan Harper Nichols, artist, poet **@MorganHarperNichols**
Naomi and Natalie Evans, writers, educators **@EverydayRacism**
National Trust, protecting nature, beauty and history **@NationalTrust**
Nicola Rae Wickham, coach **@NicolaRaeWickham**
Nova Reid, activist, anti-racism expert **@NovaReidOfficial**
OCD charity **@OCDUKCharity**
St. Mark's MK, church **@StMarksMK**
Story Gatherings, storytelling conference **@StoryGatherings**
The Bible Project, nonprofit animation studio **@TheBibleProject**
The Field, Christian camping holiday **@TheField_LA**
Vean Ima, poet **@Vean_Ima**

Deborah Fielding is a writer and artist. You can find her at withnarrative.com and on Instagram @withnarrative.

St Mark's Milton Keynes is a church defined by faith, hope and love. You can find them at stmarksmk.com.